ILLNESS

– CAUSES & CURE

Compiled by Vijay from the writings of
Sri Aurobindo and the Mother

SRI AUROBINDO SOCIETY
Pondicherry

Yoga in Everyday Life – Booklet Series

Rs. 20.00
ISBN 978-81-7060-111-1

First Centenary Edition: 1972
Fourth Revised Edition: 1996
Eighth Impression: 2009

Published by Sri Aurobindo Society, Pondicherry
Website: www.sriaurobindosociety.org.in
Printed in India at Sri Aurobindo Ashram Press, Pondicherry

This is one in a series of thirty booklets published by the Sri Aurobindo Society under the title "Yoga in Everyday Life." Our effort is to bring together, from Sri Aurobindo and the Mother, simple passages with a practical orientation on specific subjects, so that everyone may feel free to choose a book according to his inner need. The topics cover the whole field of human activity, because true spirituality is not the rejection of life but the art of perfecting life.

While the passages from Sri Aurobindo are in the original English, most of the passages from the Mother (selections from her talks and writings) are translations from the original French. We must also bear in mind that the excerpts have been taken out of their original context and that a compilation, in its very nature, is likely to have a personal and subjective approach. A sincere attempt, however, has been made to be faithful to the vision of Sri Aurobindo and the Mother.

We hope these booklets will inspire the readers to go to the complete works and will help them to mould their lives and their enviornments towards an ever greater perfection. The quotations from Sri Aurobindo are prefaced by his symbol and those from the Mother by her symbol.

The Mother's   Sri Aurobindo's

"O TRUTH, COME, MANIFEST."

"आयाहि सत्य आविर्भव"

CONTENTS

THE CAUSES OF ILLNESS

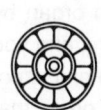 I have told you first of all that all illness without any exception – without exception – is the expression of a break in equilibrium. But there are many kinds of breaks in equilibrium.... First, I am speaking only of the body, I am not speaking of the nervous illnesses of the vital or of mental illnesses. We shall see that later on. We are speaking only of this poor little body. And I say that all illnesses, all, whatever they may be (I would add even accidents) come from a break in equilibrium. That is, if all your organs, all the members and parts of your body are in harmony with one another, you are in perfect health. But if there is the slightest imbalance anywhere, immediately you get either just a little ill or quite ill, even very badly ill, or else an accident occurs. That always happens whenever there is an inner imbalance.

But then, to the equilibrium of the body, you must add the equilibrium of the vital and the mind. For you to be able to do all kinds of things with immunity, without any accident happening to you, you must have a triple equilibrium – mental, vital, physical – and not only in each of the parts, but also in the three parts in their mutual relations.... If you have done a little mathematics, you should have been taught how many combinations that makes and what a difficult thing it means! There lies the key to the problem. For the combinations are innumerable, and conse- quently the causes of illness too are innumerable, the causes of accidents also are innumerable. Still, we are going to try to classify them so that we may understand.

Functional and Organic Causes

First of all, from the point of view of the body – just the body – there are two kinds of disequilibrium: functional and organic. I do

1

not know if you are aware of the difference between the two; but you have organs and then you have all the parts of your body: nerves, muscles, bones and all the rest. Now, if an organ by itself is in disequilibrium, it is an organic disequilibrium, and you are told: that organ is ill or perhaps it is badly formed or it is not normal or an accident has occurred to it. But it is the organ that is ill. But the organ may be in a very good condition, all your organs may be in a very good condition, but there is still an illness as they do not function properly: there is a lack of balance in the functioning. You may have a very good stomach, but suddenly something happens to it and it does not function properly; or the body may also be excellent, but something happens to it and it does not work properly any more. Then you have an illness due to functional imbalance not organic imbalance.

Generally, illnesses due to functional imbalance are cured much more quickly and easily than the others. The others become a little more serious. Sometimes they become very grave. So there are already two domains to see and know, but if you have a little knowledge of your body and the habit of observing its working, you can know what kind of imbalance yours is.

Most often when you are young and leading a normal life, the imbalance is purely functional. There are only a few poor people who for one reason or other have had an accident or imbalance before their birth, these carry with them something that is much more difficult to cure (not that it is incurable; in theory, there is nothing incurable), but it becomes more difficult.

Good. Now what are the causes of this imbalance, whatever it may be? As I told you just now, the causes are innumerable; because, first of all, there are all the inner causes, that is, those personal to you, and then all the external causes, those that come to you from outside. That makes two major categories.

The Internal Causes

We said: you have a brain, lungs, a heart, a stomach, a liver, etc. If each one does its duty and works normally and if all move together in harmony at a given moment and in the right way (note that it would be very complicated if you were obliged to think of all that, and I am afraid things would not go right all the time! Fortunately, it does not need our conscious thinking), admitting however they are in good harmony with one another, good friends, in perfect agreement, and each one fulfilling its task, its movement at the right time, in tune with the rest, neither too soon nor too late, neither too fast nor too slow, indeed, every one going all right, then you are marvellously well! Suppose now that one of them, for some reason or other, happens to be in a bad mood: it does not work with the necessary energy, at the required moment it goes awhile on strike. Do not believe that it alone will fall ill: the whole system will go wrong and you will feel altogether unwell. And if, unfortunately, there is a vital imbalance, that is, a disappointment or too violent an emotion or too strong a passion or something else upsetting your vital, that comes in addition. And if furthermore your thoughts roam about and you begin to have dark ideas and formulate frightful things and make catastrophic formations, then after that you are sure to fall ill altogether.... You see the complication, don't you, just a tiny thing can go the wrong way and thus through an inner contagion can lead to something very serious. So what is important is to control things immediately. One must be conscious, conscious of the working of one's organs, aware of the one that does not behave very well, telling it immediately what is to be done to set itself right. What is needed (I shall explain it to you later on) is to give them a lesson as one does to little children. When they begin indulging in unhealthy fancies (indeed it is then the occasion to say it) you must tell them: no, it is not like that the work is to be done, it is the other way! Suppose for example, your heart begins to throb madly; then you must make it calm, you tell it that this is not the way to act, and at the same time (solely to help it) you take in long very regular rhythmic breaths, that is, the lung becomes the mentor of the heart and teaches it how to work properly. And so on. I could give you countless examples.

Good. We say then that there is an imbalance between the different parts of the being, disharmony in their working. That is what I have just told you. And then there are internal conflicts. These are quarrels. There are internal quarrels among the different parts of yourself. Supposing there is an organ (it happens very often) that needs rest and there is another that wants action, and both at the same time. How are you going to manage it? They begin to quarrel. If you do what one wants, the other protests! And so you have to find a middle term to put them in harmony. And then, at times, if you add to the physical the vital and mental (I do not speak of the speculative mind or the independent vital, I am speaking of the mental and vital parts of the *body*, because there is a physical vital and a physical mind; there is a physical mind and this physical mind is the worst of all, it is that which goes on all the time and you have the utmost difficulty in stopping it: it goes on and on and on); well, if there is a dispute between them, between the mind, the vital and the physical, you have a battlefield, and this battlefield can become the cause of all possible illnesses. They fight violently. One wants something, the other does not, they quarrel and you are in a kind of internal whirlwind. That can give you fever – you do get it usually – or else you are seized by an inner shivering and you have no longer any control. For the most important of all causes for bodily illness is that the body begins to get restless; it trembles and the trembling increases more and more, more and more and you feel that you will never be able to re-establish the balance, it eludes you. Then in that case you must know what the dispute is about, the reason of the dispute and find out how to reconcile the people within you.

All these are functional imbalances.

There are other kinds of imbalance and they are more or less a part of what you were saying just now. There is an aspiration within you (I am now speaking of people who do yoga or at any rate know what the spiritual life is and try to walk on the path), within you there is a part of the being – either mental or vital or something even physical – that has understood well, has much aspiration, its special aptitudes, that receives the forces well and is making good progress. And then there are others that cannot, others still that don't want to (that of course is very bad), but there are yet others that want to very much but cannot, do not have the capacity, are not ready. So there is something that rises upward and something that does not move. That causes a terrible imbalance. And usually this translates itself into some illness or other, for you are in such a state of inner tension between something that cannot or something that clings, that does not want to move and something else that wants to: that produces a frightful unease and the result usually is an illness.

Now there is the opposite, almost the opposite, that is, the whole being goes ahead, progresses, advances in an increasing equilibrium and achieves remarkable progress; you have the feeling you are in a wonderfullly favourable state, everything is going on well, you are sure; and you see yourself already gloriously well on the way.... Crack! an illness. Then you say: "How is it? I was in such a good condition and now I have fallen ill! It is not fair." But this happens because you are not completely conscious. There was a small part in the being that did not want to move. Usually it is something in the vital; sometimes it is a tiny mental formation that does not agree to follow;

5

sometimes it is simply something in the body which is quite inert or has not the slightest intention of moving, that wants things to remain always as they are. It pulls backward, separates itself wilfully, and naturally, even if it is quite small, it brings about such an imbalance in the being that you fall ill. And then you say to yourself: "It is truly a pity, I was going on so well, it is not fair! Truly God is not kind!... When I was making so much progress, He ought to have prevented me from becoming ill!"... It is like that.

Now, there is still another thing. You do the yoga according to your capacity. You have been told: "Open yourself, you will receive the Force." You have been told: "Have faith, be of goodwill and you will be protected." And indeed you are bathed in the Consciousness, bathed in the Force, bathed in the Protection and to the extent you have faith and open yourself, you receive all that, and it helps you in keeping fit and in rejecting the little inner disturbances and re-establishing order when these come, in protecting yourself against small attacks or accidents which might have happened. But if somewhere in your being – either in your body or even in your vital or mind, either in several parts or even in a single one – there is an incapacity to receive the descending Force, this acts like a grain of sand in a machine. You know, a fine machine working quite well with everything going all right, and you put into it just a little sand (nothing much, only a grain of sand), suddenly everything is damaged and the machine stops. Well, just a little lack of receptivity somewhere, something that is unable to receive the Force, that is completely shut up (when one looks at it, it becomes as it were a little dark spot somewhere, a tiny thing hard as a stone: the Force cannot enter into it, it refuses to receive it – either it cannot or it will not) and immediately that produces a great imbalance; and this thing that was moving upward, that was blooming so wonderfully, finds itself sick, and sometimes just when you were in the normal equilibrium, you

6

were in good health, everything was going on well, you had nothing to complain about. One day when you grasped a new idea, received a new impulse, when you had a great aspiration and received a great force and had a marvellous experience, a beautiful experience opening to you inner doors, giving you a knowledge you did not have before; then you were sure that everything was going to be all right.... The next day, you are taken ill. So you say: "Still that? It is impossible! That should not happen." But it was quite simply what I have just said: a grain of sand. There was something that could not receive; immediately it brings about a disequilibrium. Even though very small it is enough, and you fall ill.

You see there are reasons! – many reasons, numberless reasons. For all these things combine in an extraordinarily complex way, and in order to know, in order to be able to cure an illness, one must find out its cause, not its microbe. For it happens that (excuse me, I hope there are no doctors here!), it happens that when microbes are there, they find out magnificent remedies to kill the microbes, but these remedies cure some and make others much more ill! Nobody knows why.... Perhaps I know why. Because the illness had another cause than the purely physical one; there was another; the first was only an outer expression of a different disorder; and unless you touched that, discovered that disorder, never would you be able to prevent the illness from coming. And to discover the disorder, you must have an extensive occult knowledge and also a deep knowledge of all the inner workings of each one.

External Causes

Thus we have seen in brief, very rapidly all the internal causes. Now there are external causes that come and bring complications.

If you were in a perfectly harmonious environment where everything was full of a total and perfect goodwill, then evidently you could lay the blame only on yourself. But the difficulties that are within are also without. You can, to a certain extent, establish an inner equilibrium, but you live in surroundings full of imbalance. Unless you shut yourself up in an ivory tower (which is not only difficult but not always recommendable), you are obliged to receive what comes from outside. You give and you receive; you breathe in and absorb. So there is a mixture and that is why one can say that all is contagious, for you live in a state of ceaseless vibrations. You give out your vibrations and receive also the vibrations of others, and these vibrations are of a very complex kind. There are still (we shall say for simplifying the language) mental vibrations, vital vibrations, physical vibrations and many others. You give, you receive; you give, you receive. It is a perpetual play. Even granting that there is no bad will, there is necessarily contagion. And as I was saying just now, all is contagious, everything. You are looking at the effect of an accident: you absorb a certain vibration. And if you are over-sensitive and over and above that you have fear or disgust (which is the same thing, disgust is only a moral expression of a physical fear), the accident can be translated physically in your body. Naturally you will be told that it is persons in a state of nervous imbalance who have such reactions. It is not quite that. They are persons with an ultra-suprasensitive vital, that is all. And it is not always a proof of inferiority, on the contrary! For as you progress spiritually, a certain hypersensitiveness of nerves occurs and if your self-control does not increase along with your sensibility, all kinds of untoward things may happen to you.

But that is not the only thing.

Unhappily there is much bad will in the world; and among the different kinds of bad will there is the small type that comes from

8

ignorance and stupidity, there is the big type that comes from wickedness and there is the formidable one that is the result of anti-divine forces. So, all that is in the atmosphere (I am not telling you this to frighten you, for it is well understood that one should fear nothing – but it is there all the same) and these things attack you, sometimes intentionally, sometimes unintentionally. Unintentionally, through other people: others are attacked, they don't know, they pass it on without even being aware of it. They are the first victims. They pass the illness to others. But there are wilful attacks. We were speaking the other day of mental formations and of wicked people who make mental formations to harm you, make them wilfully to do harm. And then there are others who go still a step further.

Occult Causes

There is a misguided, perverted occultism which is called black magic, it is a thing one must never touch. But unfortunately, there are people who touch it through pure wickedness. You must not believe it is an illusion, a superstition: it is real. There are people who know how to do magic and do it, and with their magic they obtain altogether detestable results.... It is understood of course that when you have no fear and remain under protection, you are sheltered. But there is a "when", there is a condition, and then if the condition is not always fulfilled, very unpleasant things may happen. So long as you are in a state full of strength, full of purity – that is, in a state of invincibility, if anybody does anything against you, that falls back upon him automatically, as when you throw a tennis-ball against the wall, it comes back to you; the thing comes back to them exactly in the same way, sometimes with a greater force, and they are punished by the very thing through which they sinned. But naturally it all depends on the person against whom the magic is done, on his inner force and purity.... These things I have known, many cases like this. And in such cases, in order to resist, one must be, as I said, a warrior in the vital, that is, a spiritual fighter in the vital. All who do yoga sincerely must become that, and when they do become that, they are altogether sheltered. But one of the conditions for becoming it is never to have bad will or a bad thought towards others. For if you have a bad feeling or bad will or a bad thought, you come down to their level and when you are on the same level with them, well, you may receive blows from them.

Now, without going to that extreme, there are in the physical atmosphere, the earth-atmosphere, numerous small entities which you do not see, for your sight is too limited, but which move about in your atmosphere. Some of them are quite nice, others very wicked. Generally these little entities are produced by the disintegration of vital beings – they pullulate – and these form quite an unpleasant mass. There are some which do very fine things. I believe I narrated to you the story of the little beings who tugged at my sari to tell me that the milk was about to boil and that I had to go and see that it did not boil over. But all of them are not so good. Some of them like to play ugly little tricks, wicked little pranks. And so most often it is they who are behind an accident. They like little accidents, they like the whole whirl of forces that gather round an accident: a mass of people, you know, it is very amusing! And then that gives them their food, because, in reality, they feed upon human vitality thrown out of the body by emotions and excitements. So they say: just a small accident, it is quite nice, many accidents!...

And then if there is a group of such small entities, they may clash with one another, because among themselves they do not have a very peaceful life: clashing with one another, fighting, destroying, demolishing each other. And that is the origin of microbes. They are forces of disintegration. But they continue to be alive even in their divided forms and this is the origin of germs and microbes. Therefore most microbes have behind them a bad will and that is what makes them so dangerous. And unless one knows the quality and kind of bad will and is capable of acting upon it, there is a ninety-nine per cent chance of not finding the true and total remedy. The microbe is a very material expression of something living in a subtle physical world and that is why these very microbes... that are always around you, within you, for years together do not make you ill and then suddenly they make you fall ill.

There is another reason. The origin of the microbes and their support lie in a disharmony, in the being's receptivity to the adverse force. I will tell you a story. I do not know whether I have already told it to you, but I am going to tell you now for it will give you an illustration.

I was in Japan. It was at the beginning of January 1919. Anyway, it was the time when a terrible flu raged there in the whole of Japan, which killed hundreds of thousands of people. It was one of those epidemics the like of which is rarely seen. In Tokyo, every day there were hundreds and hundreds of new cases. The disease appeared to take this turn: it lasted three days and on the third day the patient died. And people died in such large numbers that they could not even be cremated, you understand, it was impossible, there were too many of them. Or otherwise, if one did not die on the third day, at the end of seven days one was altogether cured; a little exhausted but all the same completely cured. There was a panic in the town, for epidemics are very rare in Japan. They are a very clean people, very careful and with a fine morale. Illnesses are very rare. But still this came, it came as a catastrophe. There was a terrible fear. For example, people were seen walking about in the streets with a mask on the nose, a mask to purify the air they were breathing, so that it might not be full of the microbes of the illness. It was a common fear.... Now, it so happened I was living with someone who never ceased troubling me: "But what is this disease? What is there behind this disease?" What I was doing, you know, was simply to cover myself with my force, my protection so as not to catch it and I did not think of it any more and continued doing my work. Nothing happened and I was not thinking of it. But constantly I heard: "What is this? Oh, I would like to know what is there behind this illness. But could you not tell me what this illness is, why it is there?..." etc. One day I was called to the other end of the town by a young woman whom I knew and who wished to introduce me to some friends and show me certain things: I do not remember now what exactly was the matter, but anyway I had to cross the whole town in a tram-car. And I was in the tram and seeing these people with masks on their noses, and then there was in the atmosphere this constant fear, and so there came a suggestion to me; I began to ask myself: "Truly, what is this illness? What is there behind this illness? What are the forces that are in this illness?..." I came to the house, I passed an hour there and I returned. And I returned with a terrible fever. I had caught it. It came to you thus, without preparation, instantaneously. Illnesses, generally illnesses from germs and microbes take a few days in the system: they come, there is a little battle inside; you win or you lose, if you lose you catch the illness, it is not complicated. But there, you just receive a letter, open the envelope, hop! puff! The next minute you have the fever. Well, that evening I had a terrible fever. The doctor was called (it was not I who called him), the doctor was called and he told me: "I must absolutely give you this medicine." It was one of the best medicines for the fever, he had just a little (all their stocks were exhausted, everyone was taking it); he said: "I have still a few packets, I shall give you some" – "I beg of you, do not give it to me, I won't take it. Keep it for someone who has faith in it and will take it." He was quite disgusted: "It was no use my coming here." So I said: "Perhaps it was no use!" And I remained in my bed, with my fever, a violent fever. All the while I was asking myself: "What is this illness? Why is it there? What is there behind it?..." At the end of the second day, as I was lying all alone, I saw clearly a being, with a part of the head cut off, in a military uniform (or the remains of a military uniform) approaching me and suddenly flinging himself upon my chest, with that half a head to suck my force. I took a good look, then realised that I was about to die. He was drawing all my life out (for I must tell you that people were dying of pneumonia in three days). I was completely nailed to the bed, without movement, in a deep trance. I could no longer stir and he was pulling. I thought: now it is the end. Then I called on my occult power, I gave a big fight and I succeeded in turning him back so that he could not stay there any longer. And I woke up.

But I had seen. And I had learnt, I had understood that the illness originated from beings who had been thrown out of their bodies. I had seen this during the First Great War, towards its end, when people used to live in trenches and were killed by bombardment. They were in perfect health, altogether healthy and in a second they were thrown out of their bodies, not conscious that they were dead. They did not know they hadn't a body any more and they tried to find in others the life they could not find in themselves. That is, they were turned into so many countless vampires. And they vampirised upon men. And then over and above that, there was a decomposition of the vital forces of people who fell ill and died. One lived in a kind of sticky and thick cloud made up of all that. And so those who took in this cloud fell ill and usually got cured, but those who were attacked by a being of that kind invariably died, they could not resist. I know how much knowledge and force were necessary for me to resist. It was irresistible. That is, if they were attacked by a being

13

who was a centre of this whirl of bad forces, they died. And there must have been many of these, a very great number. I saw all that and I understood.

When someone came to see me, I asked to be left alone, I lay quietly in my bed and I passed two or three days absolutely quiet, in concentration, with my consciousness. Subsequently, a friend of ours (a Japanese, a very good friend) came and told me: "Ah! you were ill? So what I thought was true.... Just imagine, for the last two or three days, there hasn't been a single new case of illness in the town and most of the people who were ill have been cured and the number of deaths has become almost negligible, and now it is all over. The illness is wholly under control." Then I narrated what had happened to me and he went and narrated it to everybody. They even published articles about it in the papers.

Well, consciousness, to be sure, is more effective than packets of medicines!... The condition was critical. Just imagine, there were entire villages where everyone had died. There was a village in Japan, not very big, but still with more than a hundred people, and it happened, due to an extraordinary chance, that one of the villagers was to receive a letter (the postman went there only if there was a letter; naturally, it was a village far in the countryside); so he went to the countryside; there was a snowfall; the whole village was under snow... and there was not a living person. It was exactly so. It was that kind of epidemic. And Tokyo was also like that; but Tokyo was a big town and things did not happen in the same fashion. And it was in this way the epidemic ended. That is my story....

*

With the causes you have told us about, one should be always ill!

But in ordinary life, most of the time, people are almost always ill – except a few who escape for reasons of a different order that we shall explain one day. There are very few people who are not more or less ill all the while. But even in ordinary life, if within you there is trust, goodwill, a kind of certitude, this kind of inner confidence, oh! as there is in most children perhaps (I do not know, for, after all, those we see here are fairly exceptional), however, there is a trust in life, they are young and they have the feeling that the whole life is before them. Very few things are behind, everything is in front. So that gives them a kind of self-confidence, that pulls them out.

Otherwise, I do not know, in the ordinary life I have known very few people who did not complain of having at least some physical ailment which they carried always with them.... You know perhaps that play of Jules Romains, *Doctor Knock*, in which he says that a healthy man is a sick fellow who is unaware. It is usually true. When you are sufficiently busy not to be all the while occupied with yourself, you do not notice it, but it is there.

ILLNESS AND FEAR

From the ordinary point of view, in most cases, it is usually fear – fear, which may be mental fear, vital fear, but which is almost always physical fear, a fear in the cells – it is fear which opens the door to all contagion. Mental fear – all who have a little control over themselves or any human dignity can eliminate it; vital fear is more subtle and asks for a greater control; as for physical fear, a veritable yoga is necessary to overcome it, for the cells of the body are afraid of everything that is unpleasant, painful, and as soon as there is any unease, even if it is insignificant, the cells of the body become anxious, they don't like to be uncomfortable. And then, to overcome that, the control of a conscious will is necessary. It is usually this kind of fear that opens the door to illnesses. And I am not speaking of the first two types of fear which, as I said, any human being who wants to be human in the noblest sense of the word, must overcome, for that is cowardice. But physical fear is more difficult to overcome; without it even the most violent attacks could be repelled. If one has a minimum of control over the body, one can lessen its effects, but that is not immunity. It is the kind of trembling of material, physical fear in the cells of the body which aggravates all illnesses.

Some people are spontaneously free from fear even in their body; they have a sufficient vital equilibrium in them not to be afraid, not to fear, and a natural harmony in the rhythm of their physical life which enables them to reduce the illness spontaneously to a minimum. There are others, on the other hand, with whom the thing always becomes as bad as it can be, sometimes to the point of catastrophe. There is the whole range and this can be seen quite easily. Well, this depends on a kind of happy rhythm of the movement of life in them, which is either harmonious enough to resist external attacks of illness or else doesn't exist or is not sufficiently powerful, and is replaced by that trembling of fear, that kind of instinctive anguish which transforms the least unpleasant contact into something painful and harmful. There is the whole range, from someone who can go through the worst contagion and epidemics without ever catching anything to one who falls ill at the slightest chance. So naturally it always depends on the constitution of each person; and as soon as one wants to make an effort for progress, it naturally depends on the control one has acquired over oneself, until the moment when the body becomes the docile instrument

16

of the higher Will and one can obtain from it a normal resistance to all attacks.

But when one can eliminate fear, one is almost in safety. For example, epidemics, or so-called epidemics, like those which are raging at present – ninety-nine times out of a hundred they come from fear: a fear, then, which even becomes a mental fear in its most sordid form, promoted by newspaper articles, useless talk and so on.

*

 My advice is not to worry. The more you think of it, the more you concentrate upon it and, above all, the more you fear, the more you give a chance for the thing to grow.

If, on the contrary, you turn you attention and your interest elsewhere you increase the possibilities of cure.

*

 If you are ill, your illness is looked after with so much anxiety and fear, you are given so much care that you forget to take help from the One who can help you and you fall into a vicious circle and take a morbid interest in your illness.

*

 You must not fear. Most of your troubles come from fear. In fact, ninety per cent of illnesses are the result of the subconscient fear of the body. In the ordinary consciousness of the body there is a more or less hidden anxiety about the consequences of the slightest physical disturbance. It can be translated by these words of doubt about the future: "And what will happen?" It is this anxiety

17

that must be checked. Indeed this anxiety is a lack of confidence in the Divine's Grace, the unmistakable sign that the consecration is not complete and perfect.

As a practical means of overcoming this subconscient fear each time that something of it comes to the surface, the more enlightened part of the being must impress on the body the necessity of an entire trust in the Divine's Grace, the certitude that this Grace is always working for the best in our self as well as in all, and the determination to submit entirely and unreservedly to the Divine's Will.

The body must know and be convinced that its essence is divine and that if no obstacle is put in the way of the Divine's working, nothing can harm us. This process must be steadily repeated until all recurrence of fear is stopped. And then even if the illness succeeds in making its appearance, its strength and duration will be considerably diminished until it is definitively conquered.

*

 When physical disorder comes, one must not be afraid; one must not run away from it, must face it with courage, calmness, confidence, with the certitude that illness is a *falsehood* and that if one turns entirely, in full confidence, with a complete quietude to the divine grace, it will settle in these cells as it establishes itself in the depths of the being, and the cells themselves will share in the eternal Truth and Delight.

*

 If you want to get cured there are two conditions. First you must be without fear, absolutely fearless, you understand, and secondly you must have a complete faith in the Divine protection. These two things are essential.

HOW TO CURE AN ILLNESS

 Now this brings us naturally to the cure. All that is very well, we now have the knowledge; so, how to prevent illnesses from coming, first of all, and when the illness does occur, how to cure it?

One may try ordinary means and sometimes that succeeds. It is usually when the body is convinced that it has been given the conditions under which it must be all right; it takes the resolution that it must be all right and it is cured. But if your body has not the will, the resolution to get cured, you may try whatever you like, it won't be cured. This also I know by experience. For I knew people who could be cured in five minutes, even of a disease considered very serious, and I knew people who had no fatal illness, but cherished it with such persistence that it did become fatal. It was impossible to persuade their body to let go their illness.

And it is here that one must be very careful and look at oneself with great discrimination to discover the small part in oneself that – how to put it? – takes pleasure in being ill. Oh! there are many reasons. There are people who are ill out of spite, there are people who are ill out of hate, there are people who are ill through despair, there are people... And these are not formidable movements: it is quite a small movement in the being: one is vexed and says: "You will see what is going to happen, you will see the consequences of what he has done to me! Let it come! I am going to be ill." One does not say it openly to oneself, for one would scold oneself, but there is something somewhere that thinks in that way.

So there are two things you have to do when you have discovered the disorder, big or small – the disharmony. Firstly, we said that this disharmony creates a kind of tremor and a lack of peace in the physical being, in the body. It is a kind of fever. Even if it is not a fever in general, there is localised fever; there are people who get restless. So the first thing to do is to quieten oneself, bring peace, calm, relaxation, with a total confidence, in this little corner (not necessarily in the whole body). Afterwards you see what is the cause of the disorder. You look. Of course, there are many, but still you try to find out approximately the cause of this disorder, and through the pressure of light and knowledge and spiritual force you re-establish the harmony, the proper functioning. And if the ailing part is receptive, if it does not offer any obstinate resistance, you can be cured in a few seconds.

It is not always the case. Sometimes there is, as I have said, a bad will: you are more or less on strike, at least you want the illness to have its consequences. So, that takes a little more time. However, if you do not happen to be particularly ill-willed, after some time the Force acts: after a few minutes or hours or at the most some days you are cured.

Now, in the case of special attacks of adverse forces, the things get complicated, because you have not only to deal with the will of the body (note that I do not admit the argument of those who say: ''But as for myself I do not want to be ill!'', for your consciousness always says that it does not want to be ill, one must be half-crazy to say, ''I want to be ill''; but it is not your consciousness that wants to be ill, it is some part of your body or at the most, a fragment of the vital that has gone wrong and wishes to be ill, and unless you observe with a good deal of attention you do not notice it). But I say that the situation gets complicated if behind this there is an attack, a pressure from adverse forces who really want to harm you. You may have opened the door through spiritual error, through a movement of vanity, of anger, of hatred or of violence; even if it is merely a movement that comes and goes, that can open the door. There are always germs watching and only waiting for an occasion. That is why one should be very careful. Anyhow, for some reason or other, the influence has pierced through the shell of protection and acts there encouraging the illness to become as bad as it can be. In that case the first means is not quite sufficient. Then you have to add something; you must add the Force of spiritual purification which is such an absolutely perfectly constructive force that nothing that's in the least destructive can survive there. If you have this Force at your disposal or if you can ask for it and get it, you direct it on the spot and the adverse force usually runs away immediately, for if it happens to be in the midst of this Force it gets dissolved, it disappears; for no force of disintegration can survive within this Force; therefore disintegration disappears and with it that also disappears. It can be changed into a constructive force, that is possible, or it may be simply dissolved and reduced to nothing. And with that not only is the illness cured, but all possibility of its return is also eliminated. You are cured of the illness once for all, it never comes back. There you are.

Now, all that is seen on the whole; on the details could be written books and books. I have given you only general explanations.

*

 There are two ways of curing an illness spiritually. One consists in putting a force of consciousness and truth on the physical spot which is affected. In this case the effect produced depends naturally on the receptivity of the person. Supposing the person is receptive; the force of consciousness is put upon the affected part and its pressure restores order. Many of you here can tell how Sri Aurobindo cured them. It was like a hand which came and took away the pain. It is as clear as that.

In other cases, if the body lacks receptivity altogether or if its receptivity is insufficient, one sees the inner correspondence with the psychological state which has brought about the illness and acts on that. But if the cause of the illness is refractory, not much can be done. Let us say the origin is vital. The vital absolutely refuses to change, it clings terrifically to the condition in which it is; then that is hopeless. You put the force, and usually it provokes an increase in the illness, produced by the resistance of the vital which did not want to accept anything. I speak of the vital but it can be the mind or something else.

When the action is directly upon the body, that is, on the affected part, it is possible that one is relieved; then, some hours later or even after a few days, the illness returns. This means that the cause has not been changed, that the cause is in the vital and is still there; it is only the effect which has been cured. But if one can act simultaneously upon both the cause and the effect, and the cause is sufficiently receptive to consent to change, then one is completely cured, once for all.

*

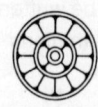 Now, quite recently, they have found something else and I consider it wonderful. They have discovered that for every disease there is a microbe that cures it (call it a microbe if you like, anyway, some sort of germ). But what is so extraordinary is that this "microbe" is extremely contagious, even more contagious than the microbe of the disease. And it generally develops under two conditions: in those who have a sort of natural good humour and energy and in those who have a strong will to get well! Suddenly they catch the "microbe" and are cured. And what is wonderful is that if there is one who is cured in an epidemic, three more recover immediately. And this "microbe" is found in all who are cured.

But I am going to tell you something: what people take to be a microbe is simply the materialisation of a vibration or a will from another world. When I learned of these medical discoveries, I said to myself, "Truly, science is making progress." One might almost say with greater reason, "Matter is progressing," it is becoming more and more receptive to a higher will. And what is translated in their science as "microbes" will be perceived, if one goes to the root of things, as simply a vibratory mode; and this vibratory mode is the material translation of a higher will. If you can bring this force or this will, this power, this vibration (call it what you will) into certain given circumstances, not only will it act in you, but also through contagion around you.

*

 ...It is well known now, that there is no better cure for illnesses, whatever they are, than *air* and *sun*.

*

 Your readings are correct.
In my last note I was referring to food desires. Unless you control the food you take, you will always be ill.

ROLE OF WILL, PEACE AND FAITH

 The body should reject illness as energetically as we reject falsehood in the mind.

*

 Do not love your ill health and the ill health will leave you.

*

The body is cured if it has decided to be cured.

*

 Wake up in yourself a will to conquer. Not a mere will in the mind but a will in the very cells of your body. Without that you can't do anything; you may take a hundred medicines but they won't cure you unless you have a will to overcome the physical illness.

*

 Both the things are correct. You must put a strong will for getting rid of your illness and you must remain quiet and unperturbed by the results. The two are not contradictory. One should accompany the other. When you are completely cured, it will be an indication of some inner progress.

*

 The only thing I can suggest about diseases is to call down peace. Keep the mind away from the body by whatever means – whether by reading Sri Aurobindo's books or meditation. It is in this state that the Grace acts. And it is the Grace alone that cures. The medicines only give a faith to the body. That is all.

*

 I have a severe pain in my throat, neck and the back of my head. The attacks are intolerable and I am losing patience.

You must not lose patience, this does not hasten the cure. On the contrary, you must keep a peaceful faith that you are going to be cured.

*

24

...if you live normally, under quite normal conditions – without having extravagant ideas and a depressing education – well, through all your youth and usually till you are about thirty, you have an absolute trust in life. If, for example, you are not surrounded by people who, as soon as you have a cold in the head, get into a flurry and rush to the doctor and give you medicines, if you are in normal surroundings and happen to have something – an accident or a slight illness – there is this certainty in the body, this absolute trust that it will be all right: "It is nothing, it will pass off. It is sure to go. I shall be quite well tomorrow or in a few days. It will surely be cured" – whatever you may have caught. That is indeed the normal condition of the body. An absolute trust that all life lies before it and that all will be well. And this helps enormously. One gets cured nine times out of ten, one gets cured very quickly with this confidence: "It is nothing; what is it after all? Just an accident, it will pass off, it is nothing." And there are people who keep it for a very long time, a very long time, a kind of confidence – nothing can happen to them. Their life is all before them, fully, and nothing can happen to them. And what will happen to them is of no importance at all: all will be well, perforce; they have the whole of life before them. Naturally, if you live in surroundings where there are morbid ideas and people pass their time recounting disastrous and catastrophic things, then you may think wrongly. And if you think wrongly, this reacts on your body. Otherwise, the body as it is can keep this confidence till the age of forty or fifty – it depends upon people – some know how to live a normal, balanced life. But the body is quite confident about its life. It is only if thought comes in and brings all kinds of morbid and unhealthy imaginations, as I said, that it changes everything....

That of course is absolute trust.

Now, you are speaking of "dynamic faith". Dynamic faith is something different. If one has within him faith in the divine grace, that the divine grace is watching over him, and that no matter what happens the divine grace is there, watching over him, this one may keep all one's life and always; and with this one can pass through all dangers, face all difficulties, and nothing stirs, for you have the faith and the divine grace is with you. It is an infinitely stronger, more conscious, more lasting force which does not depend upon the conditions of your physical build, does not depend upon anything except the divine grace alone, and hence it leans on the Truth and nothing can shake it. It is very different.

*

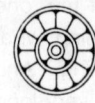 To keep quiet and to concentrate, leaving the Force from above to do its work, is the surest way to be cured of anything and everything. There is no illness that can resist that if it is done properly, in time and long enough, with a steady faith and a strong will.

*

 Finally it is Faith that cures.

*

 My dear child, now it is time for the faith to become truly active and to stand unshaken against all contradictions. Have the faith, the true faith, that you will be cured and the cure is bound to come.

*

 Instead of being upset and struggling, the best thing to do is to offer one's body to the Divine with the *sincere* prayer, "Let Thy Will be done." If there is any possibility of cure, it will establish the best

26

conditions for it; and if cure is impossible, it will be the very best preparation for getting out of the body and the life without it.

In any case the first indispensable condition is a quiet surrender to the Divine's will.

REFERENCES — ILLNESS – CAUSES & CURE

Booklet
Page

1	MCW Vol. 5, pp.173-85	23c	MCW Vol. 15, p. 159
15a	MCW Vol. 5, p. 188	d	MCW Vol. 15, p. 158
b	MCW Vol. 9, pp. 121-22	24a	MCW Vol. 15, p. 159
17a	MCW Vol. 15, p. 154	b	MCW Vol. 15, p. 158
b	MCW Vol. 15, p. 155	c	MCW Vol. 15, p. 158
c	MCW Vol. 15, p. 151	d	MCW Vol. 15, p. 161
18a	MCW Vol. 15, p. 152	e	MCW Vol. 15, p. 160
b	MCW Vol. 15, p. 152	25	MCW Vol. 5, pp. 297-98
19	MCW Vol. 5, pp. 185-88	26a	MCW Vol. 15, p. 160
21	MCW Vol. 4, pp. 264-65	b	MCW Vol. 15, p. 172
22	MCW Vol. 4, p. 210	c	MCW Vol. 15, p. 161
23a	MCW Vol. 16, p. 110	d	MCW Vol. 15, p. 161
b	MCW Vol. 15, pp. 159-60		

N.B. Abbreviations: MCW – Mother's Collected Works

The quotation in the last line of the introduction is from 'White Roses'.